# It's Spring, Arthur, Spring!

# GRAHAM

## It's Spring, Arthur, Spring!

GEOFFREY BLES

IT'S SPRING, ARTHUR, SPRING!

is published by

Geoffrey Bles, 59 Brompton Road, London SW3 1DS

ISBN 0 7138 0740 7

© Alex Graham 1973

Printed by Lewis Reprints, Tonbridge, Kent

# Contents

# Acknowledgement

These drawings originally appeared in *Punch*, and are reproduced by permission of the magazine.

# SPRING

*"Bare Winter suddenly was changed to Spring"*
**Shelley**

## IN THE GARDEN

*"Fill her up."*

# Spring—In the garden

*"Again? . . . But you only cut it yesterday!"*

*"Mickey thinks you may not have sufficient clearance between your exhaust valve stem and cam."*

"*I wonder if I could borrow a cupful of engine oil?*"

"*It's a marvellous gadget . . . you just push it along and it cuts the grass.*"

"*He took over the garage, so we put up a car-port—and now look!*"

9

## Spring—In the garden

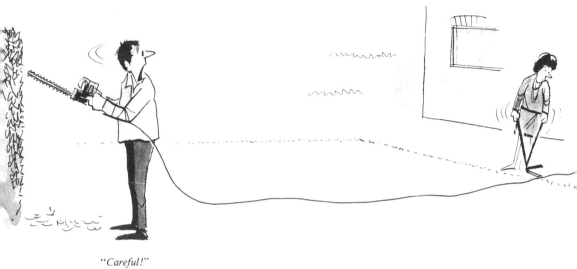

*"Careful!"*

*"Anyway, it's a start"*

*"You know you always over-do it at the beginning!"*

# WEDDING

"*So far, so good . . .*"

"*I can't go into all that now, dear!
Didn't you read that book I gave you?*"

"*Marvellous! Absolutely marvellous!*"

*"Dad, this is Robert."*

*"Am I right in thinking I have the
honour of addressing the bride's
Aunt Harriet?"*

*"At roughly four pounds a head, say,
I can't see old Charlie getting much
change out of a thousand."*

*"Few words . . . not going to bore you with long
speech . . . known Jennifer since she was a baby
. . . watched her bloom into womanhood . . .
prettiest bride ever seen . . . congratulate Robert
on his choice . . . long life and happiness
together . . . am reminded of story . . . ask you
to raise your glasses . . ."*

*"Hire department? I want to report a
nasty accident with a meringue."*

"*. . . And thanks for everything, Mr. Burton
. . . er, Dad . . . er, Pop.*"

"*I got involved in a slight fracas with one of the bridesmaids.*"

# IN THE COUNTRY

*"Noisy, smelly things!"*

*"You mean you're the only
member!"*

"We don't have much call for
it in these parts."

"It's the only way to see
the country."

*" You'll find that Amanda's
parsnip wine will happily
complement the delicate flavour
of the nut cutlet."*

*"They were just going to appoint me
Managing Director when I thought
the hell with it!"*

"*We're lost!*"

"*That'll be them hot pants we keep
hearing about.*"

"*It's a right of way.*"

*"Whatever it is, it's got black scaly wings
and lots of legs."*

*"Unless my map-reading's at fault,
just over here we should strike
the A20."*

# SUMMER

*"The Summer comes with flower and bee"*
*Felicia Dorothea Hemens*

## FÊTE

*"So a big welcome, please, for that famous and popular television star, whose name is a household word . . ."*

*"My Jennifer won it in '52."*

*"Thank you, Youth Club, for that spirited display of folk dancing . . ."*

21

"*There are others waiting, Sarah.*"

"*The Queen Mother . . . full of herself!*"

"*Boy Scouts to the tea-tent, please . . . Boy Scouts to the tea-tent, please.*"

"*I didn't know you were such a good bowler.*"

# HEAT WAVE

*"What was it like on the train?"*

*"Selfish little monkey!"*

*"Look, I think I'll skip porridge this morning."*

*"The Joneses are having disappointing weather in Malaga!"*

*"But I'll say this, Morton . . . I admire your courage!"*

## DAUGHTER ON THE BEACH

*"Don't you dare say that — Daddy looks very nice in his shorts!"*

*"Mummy, this is Tony."*

# Summer—Daughter on the beach

*"Even the damned sandwiches taste of Ambre Solaire!"*

*"Lying around here when she could be
joining in the fun!"*

*"Am I browner than Sally Gibson was when she came back from Sicily?"*

*"I think that young man's just showing off to attract her attention."*

## CAMPING

*"Could we be taking too much?"*

*"Still, look what we're saving on hotel bills."*

*"Good heavens, woman, aren't you changed yet?"*

*"By Golly, this is the life, eh?"*

*"It looked lovely when we arrived, Arthur, but now it seems sort of . . . you know . . . creepy."*

# Summer—Camping

*"Was it George and Mary Watson who did it for three whole weeks?"*

# VILLAGE CRICKET

*"Hold it! He's fainted!"* .

# Summer—Village cricket

*"Nobody else thought you'd touched it, Vicar."*

"... or Benson! You never put **him** at silly short leg!"

"You've just missed Sid Bowker's hat-trick—all retired hurt!"

# AUTUMN

*"Behold congenial Autumn comes"*
*John Logan*

## FOGBOUND

*"Good evening . . . where am I?"*

*"The trouble is you never know what some of them might be up to!"*

"BBC News? A.A. spokesman here . . . ready? . . . Chaotic conditions . . . a motorists' nightmare . . . Britain paralysed . . ."

"We're all right, Doris! . . . it's a pedestrian crossing."

"I've as much right to straddle the cat's eyes as *you* have!"

*"They've always got some excuse!"*

*"Leicester Square, guv? . . . this is Leicester Square!"*

"*And that'll teach 'em to tag on to the car in front!*"

# THE NEW MINK

*"It's lovely, dear . . . not unlike one of mine!"*

*"Did you scream?"*

"*Darling, **please** stop going on about all these poor little animals.*"

"*Oh, for heaven's sake!*"

"*Come to bed, Adèle!*"

# Autumn—The new mink

*"Damn! Another mild sunny day!"*

*"I thought it seemed a little chilly in here."*

# KICK-OFF

*"Shall we quickly run through the offside rule together?"*

*"Cramp! . . . and they're only shooting in!"*

*"I've forgotten—are we playing 4-2-4 or 3-4-3 this season?"*

*"Congratulations on your first goal of the season."*

"*God! I'm out of condition!*"

"*This new manager'll have to go!*"

"*Nobody's fainted—my friend's sprained his throwing arm.*"

# Autumn

*i*

*ii*

*iii*

*iv*

*v*

# UNIVERSITY FIRST TERM

*"Dammit, it's only a ten week term, isn't it?"*

*"She seems to be sharing a flat with
a girl called Arthur."*

*"Just in case anybody asks us . . .
what's social anthropology?"*

*"She wants a word with you about the inadequacy
of her grant."*

*"To think she won the deportment prize in her
last year at school . . ."*

49

# WINTER

*"If Winter comes can Spring be far behind"*
*Shelley*

## A TOUCH OF 'FLU

*"I'd be grateful if you'd stave it off until Dickson gets back from his."*

*"It's a mild type apparently."*

# Winter—A touch of flu

*"They say hot whisky and water works wonders."*

*"They sent a boy round with it."*

"*I think I feel strong enough to watch a little television this evening.*"

# SALE

"I'll take the lot!"

*"Probably lost her Mummy,*
*poor little thing."*

*"I've forgotten—what size do*
*you take in under-pants?"*

*"They were practically giving*
*them away."*

## BAZAAR

*"Miss!"*

*"Well done indeed, the Misses Fanshawe!"*

"*It's the half bottle of rum they all go for.*"

"*Two jiggers of gin, one of that, a twist of lemon peel, well shaken with ice . . . . delicious!*"

"*I know damned well it's in a good cause!*"

# THE FAMILY FOR CHRISTMAS

*"But is it enough, bearing in mind that your
brother Ronald's coming?"*

*"And for heaven's sake, this year try to exude
a little bonhomie."*

"*Wait a minute, wait a minute, now I've got you!
You're my brother-in-law.*"

"*She's not **my** aunt! . . . I thought she
was **your** aunt!*"

"*How about a big kiss for your
Uncle Arthur?*"

# Winter—The family for Christmas

*"Once the Queen's broadcast's out of the way, we'll get the hell out of it."*

*"Now take this Rhodesian situation."*

*"Must you go?"*

*"I wondered if we should have volunteered to help with the washing-up."*

# TOYSHOP

"*I hope he likes it.*"

"*It's for the wife, actually.*"

*"Let's club together and buy one for mummy."*

*"Two bathrooms?"*

"*We'll think it over.*"

"*Oh come along dad!*"